Praise for
Divine Discontent
by Michael Youssef, PhD

"Is it true that we all live in quiet desperation? Or can we truly sing that it is well with our souls? In *Divine Discontent,* Michael Youssef reminds us that the restlessness in our souls can actually draw us to God. By using the biographies of Scripture, Dr. Youssef illustrates that God's peace, His perfect peace, is readily available to us all. If you are looking for real rest in your spirit, Divine Discontent is *real* comfort for your restless heart."

—JANET PARSHALL, nationally syndicated talk-show host

"With characteristic clarity and conviction, Michael Youssef takes us by the hand and chapter by chapter leads us from the turbulent and often treacherous dead ends of life to the deep and settled peace that only God can give."

—DR. JOSEPH M. STOWELL, president of Moody Bible Institute and author of *The Trouble with Jesus*

Praise for
The Spirituality That Heals
by Michael Youssef, PhD

"Michael Youssef leads us out of the shadowlands of superficial spirituality into the promised land of genuine sanctifying spirituality. Prepare to be challenged and changed!"

> —HANK HANEGRAAFF, host of the *Bible Answer Man* radio
> program and author of *The Prayer of Jesus*

"In a broken, hurting world that longs for hope, Michael Youssef has provided a remedy for our souls that is both biblical and practical. Read this and embrace the healing power of God."

> —DR. JOSEPH M. STOWELL, president of Moody Bible
> Institute and author of *The Trouble with Jesus*

"Michael Youssef does an inspiring job of teaching the remarkable truth about the work of the Holy Spirit. His book will invite you to empty yourself and seek to be filled with God's Spirit."

> —NICKY CRUZ, international evangelist and author
> of *One Holy Fire* and *Run, Baby, Run*

I LONG FOR *You,* O GOD

I LONG FOR FOR *You,* OGOD

Finding Rest and Contentment
in Your Private Worship

MICHAEL YOUSSEF, PhD

WATERBROOK
PRESS

I Long for You, O God
Published by WaterBrook Press
2375 Telstar Drive, Suite 160
Colorado Springs, Colorado 80920
A division of Random House, Inc.

All Scripture quotations, unless otherwise indicated, are taken from the *Holy Bible, New International Version*®. NIV®. Copyright © 1973, 1978, 1984 by International Bible Society. Used by permission of Zondervan Publishing House. All rights reserved. Scripture quotations marked (NKJV) are taken from the *New King James Version.* Copyright © 1982 by Thomas Nelson, Inc. Used by permission. All rights reserved.

ISBN 1-57856-559-6

Library of Congress Cataloging-in-Publication Data
  Youssef, Michael.
    I long for you, O God : finding rest and contentment in your private
  worship / Michael Youssef.— 1st ed.
        p. cm.
      ISBN 1-57856-559-6
    1. Contentment—Religious aspects—Christianity. 2. Devotional
      calendars. I. Title.
    BV4647.C7Y685 2004
    248.8'6—dc22   2004015148
Printed in the United States of America
2004—First Edition

10 9 8 7 6 5 4 3 2 1

—◆—

This book is dedicated posthumously to Sam and Louisa Ayoub, two people who meant so much to me, my family, and the members of The Church of the Apostles. They have blessed the work of God around the world, and while they are in heaven, their impact goes on.

CONTENTS

OUR MISSING PEACE

Restore to me the joy of your salvation
and grant me a willing spirit, to sustain me.

PSALM 51:12

Are you convinced that if things were different, you would be happier and more at peace? Are you gaining less satisfaction from the things that consume most of your time and energy? Is there a steady background hum in your life—the dull hum of dissatisfaction?

This deep-seated discontent is not limited to those who are struggling with life's hurts and tragedies. In fact, a sense of dissatisfaction with life is often more pronounced among people who—from all outward appearances—seem to have it made. One's level of success does nothing to minimize the symptoms of discontent. The nagging inner voice continues to insist, "There has to be more. Something is *still* missing."

What lies behind our drive to find contentment? Some observers place the blame on materialism. They point out that advertising and the entertainment media have programmed us to be dissatisfied. While marketers do bear part of the blame, there is a far deeper explanation—a spiritual explanation—for our lack of contentment.

God's Word makes it clear that our lack of peace and loss of satisfaction are spiritual issues. As we study the Scriptures, we see that the loss of contentment can push us in one of two directions. The search can either lead us down paths cluttered with false promises of fulfillment, or it can bring us to a place of turning, where the journey takes on a redemptive quality. Our search for contentment can ultimately lead us to the heart of God, which is the *only* place where we will find rest and a place of belonging. It's the only place that will quiet our hearts and restore our souls.

Although the search for contentment is as current as today's news, it's also as old as humanity. Adam and Eve forfeited their contentment when they disobeyed God and ate from the forbidden tree. They were banished from the Garden, which set in motion an ongoing quest to regain the peace that had been forfeited.

Since then, men and women through the ages have sought an end to their restlessness. In his memoir, *Confessions,* written in AD 400, Augustine recounts how he overcame his lustful pursuits and found peace. In a moment of truth, he realized that there is only one solution. Explaining humankind's inborn desire to seek

God and to praise Him, Augustine wrote, "You have made us for Yourself, and our hearts are restless until they find their rest in You."[1]

There it is, in a nutshell: The place of ultimate rest is found nowhere else but in intimate relationship with the Lord. We are made in the image and likeness of our heavenly Father, and we all share an abiding need to be in close communion with Him. Every good thing that comes into our lives—whether the love of family or the beauty of God's creation or the wonder of His work in our midst—none of these will come close to quieting our restless hearts.

Why is it, then, that we insist on pursuing all the earthly "solutions" to our discontent? It seems human nature is given to restlessness, even when that means turning our back on God. The good news is that God wants to refresh our souls—to replace anxiety with peace, to give us rest in place of weariness, to provide a place of belonging that will quiet our restlessness. God wants to restore us to a place of contentment in His love and grace.

My prayer for you is that this devotional journey will give you new insight into the heart of the only One who can quiet your discontent. As you delve into His Word, submit your restless spirit to Him and experience the satisfaction that comes from an intimate relationship with the One who died on the Cross to give you peace.

---

1. Augustine, *Confessions* (New York: Oxford University Press, 1998), 1.

PART I

DEFINING OUR
DISCONTENTMENT

*Now the LORD God had planted a garden
in the east, in Eden; and there he put
the man he had formed.*

GENESIS 2:8

DAY 1

THE LOSS OF CONTENTMENT

Our lack of contentment keeps us moving—if not always geographically, at least internally. The search for contentment produces an inner restlessness, which is fed by the belief that we'll never really be satisfied where we are. We suspect the answer is just beyond the next bend in the road, and someday we'll reach our hoped-for destination. At least that's our hope.

It might seem odd that we would study an ancient Bible story to find the explanation for our modern disease of discontent. But a spiritual cause is the only explanation for our restlessness. In the book of Genesis, restlessness first appears when Adam and Eve sin against God. The shame they feel after their disobedience brings an uneasiness and an unsettledness to their life. Those traits become more than simply feelings when God casts them out of the Garden of Eden.

Although Adam and Eve were allowed to remain *near* the

ـarden, they constantly sensed their loss of intimacy with God. Their sin put distance between them and their Creator. And the same is true for us. Our sin moves us far from God and steals our contentment. To understand the implications of our sin nature, we must gain a clear picture of God's plan for humanity from beginning to end. In my view, this makes the first few chapters of the Bible critically important.

The Bible begins with Creation. As God created matter out of nothing, He set aside a special place where He fellowshiped with Adam and then with Eve. It was an incredibly beautiful garden called Eden in which Adam and Eve enjoyed unhindered communion with God. Scripture ends with the book of Revelation, which describes the New Jerusalem, a magnificent garden city that will come down from heaven. In between these two gardens, as we read the biblical account, there was a middle garden—the Garden of Gethsemane.

At the beginning, Adam and Eve were placed in the Garden as God's deputies, and Revelation depicts Jesus's followers ruling and reigning with Him. The Bible begins with a man and a woman in a place of tranquility and joy, and it ends with all believers in a place of infinite tranquility and everlasting joy.

But just as the beginning mirrors the ending, there is much that happens in between. Scripture reveals not only the cause of our restlessness, it also leads us to the perfect solution. God provides a place of peace, rest, and belonging—a place where our search for contentment comes to an end.

In the meantime, we can experience peace here and now

when we come to God through Christ, who in the Garden of Gethsemane agreed to the Father's will that He pay the penalty for Adam's sin and the sins of all who would willingly receive Him as Lord and Savior.

———◆———

Lord, as I begin this study, search my heart to reveal my restlessness. You know the motives behind my thoughts and actions. In Your Word, You promise that when I seek You, I will find You. Help me begin to trust that You alone are the source of true contentment. See 1 Chronicles 28:9

LESSONS FROM THE GARDEN

When God created humanity, there was perfect contentment. Adam and Eve lived in paradise, a place of complete peace and protection.[1] As we try to imagine what such a place was like, we gain three insights that clarify the difference between our lack of contentment and the true peace that God desires for us.

Exquisite beauty. As God created every part of the universe, He pronounced it "good." But He unleashed the full extent of His creative power when He designed a garden home for Adam and Eve. For their enjoyment, He poured out beauty beyond comprehension.

---

1. Our word *paradise* comes from a Persian word that refers to a garden or enclosed park. The same word also connotes a place of peace and protection—exactly what the Garden of Eden was designed to provide.

Abundant provision. The beauty of the Garden of Eden also was functional. The trees were pleasing to the eye but also good for food. As part of God's plan of provision, He assigned Adam the job of maintaining the Garden.

Before the Fall, Adam and Eve didn't just lounge around all day—they had work to do. "The LORD God took the man and put him in the Garden of Eden to work it and take care of it" (Genesis 2:15). They had important work to do, but they were working *inside* the Garden, in God's presence, and that made all the difference. They found fulfillment in the satisfying work that God gave them.

Complete protection. The garden's ability to protect its occupants demonstrates a third element of contentment. God sheltered Adam and Eve, guarding them from all danger. Within the garden's walls, Adam and Eve lived in an atmosphere of sweet harmony with each other and with God.

This same God longs to provide for you, protect you, and fellowship with you today. When you take time to talk with God, He will talk with you. You can know God's heart by reading His Word. And when you fellowship with Him, you have His divine protection.

———◆———

Heavenly Father, thank You for Your everlasting love and protection. I know that You desire to have a personal, daily relationship with me. Show me how I can draw closer to

You through Your Word. I long for Your fellowship and I ask for Your protection. "Keep me as the apple of Your eye; hide me under the shadow of Your wings." Psalm 17:8 (NKJV)

DECEPTION ENTERS THE GARDEN

Just as pollution despoils the environment today, sin devastated the Garden of Eden. Through man's disobedience, sin gained a foothold in God's garden and turned it into a spiritual garbage dump.

While Adam and Eve had always enjoyed complete protection in the Garden, they fell for the serpent's deception and exposed themselves to danger. In the middle of the Garden, God placed a special tree called the Tree of the Knowledge of Good and Evil, and God instructed Adam and Eve not to eat the fruit of this tree.

You are free to eat from any tree in the garden; but
you must not eat from the tree of the knowledge of

good and evil, for when you eat of it you will surely
die. (Genesis 2:16-17)

Temptation always brings a choice. It is an opportunity either
to come under God's authority and have victory or to go our own
way and suffer defeat. Alone we are helpless victims, but with the
Lord we are conquerors.

When Adam and Eve ate the forbidden fruit, their disobedience infected all of humanity with the virus of sin. But Jesus's
perfect obedience led Him from the Garden of Gethsemane to
the Cross, making it possible for His followers to be forgiven of
their sins.

In the Garden of Eden, the first man rebelled against God.
But in the Garden of Gethsemane, Jesus, the perfect God-man,
obeyed the Father fully. Satan got the upper hand in the first garden. But in the second garden, Jesus submitted to His Father's
will, which guaranteed Satan's defeat.

When Jesus prayed in the Garden of Gethsemane, He agreed
to obey His Father and sacrifice Himself on the Cross. God revealed His perfect plan to give us victory over the sin that was
born in the Garden of Eden.

If you are not walking in the power of the One who defeated
sin, then sin is defeating you. But just as one tree of temptation
held sway over Adam, it was on the tree of Calvary that Jesus was
crucified, taking back the sting of sin and death and giving us the
hope of heaven.

———◆———

Father God, help me recognize and resist the Enemy's schemes. Give me strength to emerge victorious from times of temptation. "Resist the devil, and he will flee from you." James 4:7

"The Lord knows how to deliver the godly out of temptations and to reserve the unjust under punishment for the day of judgment." 2 Peter 2:9 (NKJV)

RUNNING FROM GOD

Adam and Eve owned up to their sin, and they regretted the break in their relationship with God. But not so their son Cain.

In spite of his parents' conscientious teaching, Cain's disobedience far surpassed that of Adam and Eve. The story of how Cain murdered his brother, Abel, is familiar to us, as is the defiant question Cain asked God: "Am I my brother's keeper?" (Genesis 4:9).

Cain's anger led to the murder. He was angry that God accepted Abel's offering while rejecting his own. Cain brought an offering to the Lord from his harvest. Abel also brought an offering, the firstborn from his flock. The brothers' offerings were consistent with their occupations: Cain tilled the ground and Abel raised sheep. Outwardly, both brothers seemed to be performing a righteous act. But Cain wanted to approach God on his own terms.

The Bible doesn't specify how either brother knew whether God accepted or rejected his offering, but it's clear that they understood the outcome: "The LORD looked with favor on Abel and his offering, but on Cain and his offering he did not look with favor. So Cain was very angry, and his face was downcast" (Genesis 4:4-5). God issued a stern warning, telling Cain that sin was lying in wait for him. But God also offered mercy, making it clear that if Cain did what was right, he would be accepted. Cain refused to heed God's warning. Instead, he enticed his younger brother into a field where he beat him to death.

Unlike Adam and Eve, who first tried to make excuses for their sin in the Garden, Cain denied his sin. When God confronted him, Cain said he knew nothing about his brother's murder. As punishment, Cain had to leave the land of Eden and became "a restless wanderer on the earth" (Genesis 4:12).

Like Cain, many people today are running from God. Perhaps they are not even aware that they are wandering spiritually. But running from God will never alleviate the guilt of sin. Only one remedy exists, and that is found in facing up to our shortcomings. The way to deal with sin and guilt is through confession and repentance.

———◆———

Lord, there have been times when I have run from You. I have hidden from You because of my sin and guilt. But I am tired of living apart from Your love and protection. "Have mercy on me, O God, according to your unfailing love; according to your great compassion blot out my transgressions." Psalm 51:1

SEEKING REFUGE

Cain was given a chance to repent, but he chose instead to reject God's mercy. He tried to run from God and built his own city—and each generation of his descendants living in that city achieved a new level of wickedness. The city was filled with lonely, hard, arrogant, self-seeking people. This is because choosing a self-directed life instead of obedience to God always leads to loneliness and isolation.

Contrast this with the Garden of Eden. Fear and anxiety didn't exist there, because God was their Protector. There was no possibility of economic collapse, because God was their Provider. God intended for His people to live in the unspoiled environment of the Garden, but man chose to wander from God and build a city.

In a large city you find masses of people, of course. Yet a significant proportion of them, perhaps the majority, feel a deep sense of loneliness. Uncomfortable being alone, people tend to gather in groups, harboring the illusion that they are connected to others. But most of them share no more connection than a passing acquaintance.

Most people concentrate on their own concerns, hardly thinking of others and failing at intimacy. Even husbands and wives can feel like strangers. We are often too afraid to look in our own hearts, let alone share our thoughts and feelings with another person. Being intimate means opening up to one another and being vulnerable, and that's a risk many of us are not willing to take.

This is not the way God meant for us to live. He designed us to need each other. In the Garden, Adam and Eve fellowshiped with God—enjoying each other's company and sharing the enjoyment of their environment.

Cain did just the opposite as he deliberately put distance between himself and God. If we follow Cain's example, seeking refuge apart from the presence of God, we will never find peace. The peace we yearn for can be found only in the garden of God's grace.

———◆———

There is no place of refuge apart from You, O Lord, that will satisfy my restless heart. There is no other person, relationship, or situation that will bring lasting peace into my life. Help me walk away from the false promises of the "city of man."

Instead, show me how to put my trust in You. "Trust in the LORD with all your heart, and lean not on your own understanding; in all your ways acknowledge Him, and He shall direct your paths." Proverbs 3:5-6 (NKJV)

RESTLESS REBELLION

The inhabitants of the city of man were ruled by pride and arrogance, refusing to be accountable to anyone—least of all God. In such an amoral climate, violence runs rampant and justice is perverted.

If you believe the "gangsta" rap music of today, which glorifies violence and demeans women, is something new, you are mistaken. The mind-set that birthed this musical genre can be traced to Cain's descendants. The fourth chapter of Genesis records a song in which a vengeful Lamech boasts of inflicting violence on his enemies:

> Adah and Zillah, listen to me;
>> wives of Lamech, hear my words.
> I have killed a man for wounding me,

a young man for injuring me.

If Cain is avenged seven times,

then Lamech seventy-seven times. (Genesis 4:23-24)

In the Hebrew language, these words come across as defiance against God. Lamech might as well have been saying, "God does not run the world according to my preferences, so I've decided to take things into my own hands."

Lamech's boasting would not sound that unusual today, in a culture that tries to overthrow all vestiges of authority—especially God's authority. There is no better example of this than the U.S. Supreme Court overturning state laws prohibiting sodomy. God will not tolerate the wickedness of the city of man indefinitely. But as He executes judgment, He will preserve a godly remnant of those who stand against evil.

That's exactly what we see in Scripture:

The LORD saw how great man's wickedness on the earth had become, and that every inclination of the thoughts of his heart was only evil all the time. The LORD was grieved that he had made man on the earth, and his heart was filled with pain. So the LORD said, "I will wipe mankind, whom I have created, from the face of the earth—men and animals, and creatures that move along the ground, and birds of the air—for I am grieved that I have made them." (Genesis 6:5-7)

What an amazing proclamation—the annihilation of all living beings! Yet God is not without mercy. The very next verse says, "But Noah found favor in the eyes of the LORD" (Genesis 6:8).

We're all familiar with the story of Noah's building an ark and loading it with his family and two of every animal on earth. While God brought judgment on human wickedness, He also preserved a faithful remnant and even made gracious provision for the animal kingdom. After the majority of the earth's population was wiped out, Noah's descendants began to repopulate the planet. Yet because man retained his sin nature, peace and contentment did not prevail for long.

———◆———

Father God, I do not want to live in rebellion against You and Your will. For only when I live in obedience to You will I experience Your blessings. Reveal to me the areas of my life that displease You so that I may repent and be restored to fellowship with You. "Search me, O God, and know my heart; test me and know my anxious thoughts." Psalm 139:23

AN EXERCISE IN FUTILITY

The story of God's confusing the languages at the Tower of Babel is a familiar one. What is less familiar is the rebellion that motivated the tower's construction. A famed warrior named Nimrod attempted to build the Babylonian structure as a symbol of human effort in trying to find contentment apart from God (see Genesis 10:8-12; 11:1-9).

The Bible tells us that Nimrod was a proud and powerful king who couldn't comprehend serving anyone. So he attempted to prove that he had no need of God. In fact, he devoted his life to building a civilization in opposition to God's authority.

Although Nimrod's tower was constructed in ancient times, it might surprise you to know there is a Babylonian revival in our own time. This pagan revival has fostered a host of popular practices, including tarot cards, horoscopes, and psychic hot lines. The price tag of this growing interest in pagan spirituality is astronomical in both its financial and spiritual impact, as many people have destroyed their lives by acting on advice from psychics and shamans. If they had only sought God's counsel, if they had searched the Word of God, they could have been spared untold pain.

Nimrod's tower was, in many ways, the next step in a progression of human rebellion against God. Adam and Eve sinned but settled near the Garden of Eden, remaining close to God's presence. Cain murdered his brother and then ran from God, settling in the land of Nod. Nimrod took this progression of sin several steps further, establishing an entire civilization in opposition to God.

This same arrogant mind-set continues to rule those who refuse God's authority. Every disease and sickness, every heartache and pain, is the result of original sin. Many people reject Christ's sacrifice that can bring salvation, choosing instead to try to conquer sin's consequences on their own terms. Many believe that given enough money and time, we can do anything. We place our trust in science and supercomputers. Technology has become our god.

Nimrod's actions reflect this same attitude. He made a god of his own ambition and pride, but he found that God's decrees can't be defied for very long.

As we read the biblical account of Nimrod and the Tower of Babel, we see the danger of striving to quell our spiritual discontent outside of God's plan for humanity. The only reliable spiritual guidance available to us is God's unerring direction.

———◆———

Father, I know that I often try to do things my own way and in my own strength, without asking for Your help. I pray that You would help me realize just how much I need You. Alone I am weak, but in Your strength anything is possible. See Philippians 4:13

LIVING IN OPPOSITION
TO GOD

From Genesis to the book of Revelation, Babylon is a symbol of living at enmity with God. This dubious reputation was born when the inhabitants of Babylon said, "Come, let us build ourselves a city, with a tower that reaches to the heavens" (Genesis 11:4). With that statement, the well-organized human opposition to God began.

The implication of the Babylonians' figure of speech, "reaches the heavens," is that the top of their tower would be dedicated to the worship of the heavenly bodies. It was from Babylon that astrology, the belief that the stars and planets influence human affairs and events on earth, was passed on to the entire world.

After four hundred years of slavery in Egypt, even the Hebrews had begun to practice astrology. When the Lord brought them out of Egypt, He warned them against worshiping the stars (see Deuteronomy 18:9-13). In reality, those who look to the stars for the key to their destinies are worshiping Satan and his demonic forces.

Notice Satan's modus operandi. After he was thrown out of heaven, Satan deceived Adam and Eve into doubting God and managed to get them thrown out of the Garden. Then Satan deceived Cain into worshiping in his own way rather than God's way, which led to Abel's murder and ultimately to the massive destruction of life by the Flood. Then Satan deceived Ham's descendants into worshiping the zodiac—actually the worship of demons—thereby causing their destruction.

Satan always sows deception and confusion. He convinces people to take a gift and turn it into an idol. The Babylonians used their innate desire for self-preservation to build a monument to glorify themselves. They turned God's gift of self-protection into an idol of self-worship. When people don't worship God, they embrace false gods, intentionally or not.

———◆———

Lord, You have warned us against worshiping false gods, saying, "And when you look up to the sky and see the sun, the moon and the stars—all the heavenly array—do not be enticed into bowing down to them and worshiping things the

LORD your God has apportioned to all the nations under heaven. " Deuteronomy 4:19

Help me to avoid the temptation of looking to the world's deceptive practices for advice and counsel. Instead, turn my heart toward the truth of Your Word.

CONFRONTING OUR IDOLS

It's easy to criticize the pride and shortsightedness of the ancient Babylonians. But consider that we continue worshiping idols today, often without realizing it. The most dominant among our idols is the god of self. Our resources, our energy, our time—our complete focus—is on the self. Slick politicians make campaign speeches that cater to the powerful god of self. The advertising industry dedicates itself to feeding the god of self.

Self-esteem has become the byword in education. For all age levels, curricula is designed to increase students' self-esteem. With this emphasis on kids feeling good about themselves, however, their academic performance has failed to follow suit. The Third International Math and Science Study showed that American students performed dismally compared to students of other nations.[1]

---

1. See Dinesh D'Souza, "Education's Self-Esteem Hoax," *Christian Science Monitor,* 24 October 2002, www.csmonitor.com/2002/1024/p09s01-coop.html.

In our discontented pursuit of a "better" self, we're not that different from the Babylonians. When the Babylonian council assembled to defy God and try to steal His glory, God assembled His own council. The divine meeting I'm referring to is described in Genesis 11:6-7: "The LORD said, 'If as one people speaking the same language they have begun to do this, then nothing they plan to do will be impossible for them. Come, let us go down and confuse their language so they will not understand each other.' "

The decree issued from the Council of the Holy Trinity resulted in a massive human communication problem that prevented the tower from being completed. God's judgment always prevails, and those who continue to worship the god of self will always be frustrated and sometimes, even destroyed.

Humanity uses modern technology to build great buildings, and these towering edifices engender great pride. When you stand on the ground looking up at the Sears Tower, it literally makes you dizzy. But when you fly above that same skyscraper, it looks insignificant. From God's perspective, all of humanity's achievements amount to nothing more than a pimple on the face of the planet.

Focusing on ourselves and our abilities—whether it's self-esteem or self-actualization—will produce the opposite of the contentment that we long for. There is only one solution to our search for peace and lasting satisfaction. In the next few days, we will explore how we can find our contentment in God.

———◆———

"Therefore, my beloved, flee from idolatry." 1 Corinthians 10:14 (NKJV)

Lord, if I have allowed anything to become an idol in my life, I pray that You would reveal it to me now. I know that You warn against idolatry because of Your love for me. You want what is best for me, and that is to glorify You with all of my being.

PART II

WHERE SEARCHING LEADS US

O God, you are my God,
earnestly I seek you;
my soul thirsts for you,
my body longs for you,
in a dry and weary land
where there is no water.

PSALM 63:1

FROM THE DEPTHS OF DEPRESSION

While many men and women of the Bible sought earthly contentment apart from God, there were others whose unsettled lives ultimately drove them into the Lord's presence. Their wandering led them in the opposite direction of their ancestors. They ran *to* God instead of away from Him.

David, in all the upheaval of his life, was constantly running to God. Yet, in all his candid questions and passionate expressions of vulnerability, we don't sense that David ever lost faith in God's power to make things right. What may surprise you is that David, a man of faith, appeared to have several bouts with what modern psychologists would label depression.

Even though an estimated 10 percent of the U.S. population is affected by depressive illness at any given time,[1] Christians often

---

1. See Prentiss Price, "All About Depression," www.allaboutdepression.com.

are ashamed to admit to dark periods of despair. The life of David, however, teaches us that every person, even those who trust God, at some point enters a dark valley. In fact, almost anyone who responds to the call of God will one day face doubts and questions, difficulties and trials, that will lead him or her through the door of depression. Jeremiah was known as the "weeping prophet" because he anguished over the sins of God's people and the judgment he saw coming as a result of their disobedience. More than once he withdrew in defeat and asked God why he had even been born.

Like Jeremiah and other dedicated servants of God, David experienced a similar bout of depression (see Psalm 63). Yet his hunger for God, even in the pit of despair, is a vivid demonstration of the biblical answer to depression. If we are willing, we can turn our despair into a passionate pursuit of God. That's when the search for peace—and deliverance from the dark valley— brings us back to God's heart.

———◆———

Heavenly Father, I confess that at times I have been overwhelmed with feelings of despair. But I draw hope from the example of Your servant David, who continued to seek You even in the darkest valley. I trust in Your promise that "Those who sow in tears will reap with songs of joy." Psalm 126:5

THIRSTING FOR GOD

Psalm 42 is a beautifully poetic description of spiritual hunger, showing that the answer to our restlessness is a driving thirst for God: "As the deer pants for streams of water, so my soul pants for you, O God" (Psalm 42:1).

So it is in the moment of our deepest discouragement: relief comes only when we thirst for God.

The writer of Psalm 42 does not offer platitudes. He cuts through the pat answers and tells us that the only spring of water that will satisfy our desperate need is the Living Water. I can picture David observing an exhausted deer—spent, feverish, and desperate for water—finally reaching the edge of a stream.

David himself was desperate, as he considered the threats of his own murderous son, Absalom. For David, only the fountain of God could satisfy his spiritual thirst and alleviate his "emotional fever."

That's where we all need to be: thirsting for God. We need to stop longing for the trappings of religion and instead seek God Himself. We need to ask ourselves, are we going to church to hear a compelling sermon or beautiful, inspiring music? Are we going because of the programs and social activities?

Or are we going to meet God?

When we seek contentment in anything but God, we miss the first, most important step toward restoration: the Living Water. Only a burning thirst for God will bring satisfaction.

Notice the words that describe David's desperate longing: "My soul thirsts for God, for the living God. When can I go and meet with God?" (Psalm 42:2).

All that David could do was weep tears of pain, exhaustion, grief, and despair. There is a blessed release in tears. If we refuse tears, we are refusing a God-ordained channel of restoration. Jesus said, "Blessed are those who mourn, for they will be comforted" (Matthew 5:4).

When we are connected to Jesus, there is a balm in times of suffering. His name is a healing ointment that soothes our spirits. There are different seasons in life—times of weeping and mourning and times of laughter and dancing. If you are going through a season of sorrow, remember that "weeping may remain for a night, but rejoicing comes in the morning" (Psalm 30:5). Keep in mind that as David poured out his soul to the Lord, he reclaimed his joy.

———◆———

O God, You are my God, earnestly I seek You; my soul thirsts for You, my body longs for You "in a dry and weary land where there is no water." Psalm 63:1

Lord, I long for Your healing presence and Your peace to return to my life. I offer the deep sorrows of my heart to You now and ask for the comfort of Your Holy Spirit.

REMEMBERING
GOD'S FAITHFULNESS

In Psalm 42:4, we see David gaining encouragement by looking back: "These things I remember as I pour out my soul: how I used to go with the multitude, leading the procession to the house of God, with shouts of joy and thanksgiving among the festive throng."

David was not reluctant to abandon himself in praise to the Lord, even in front of his subjects. And as he waited in despair for word on Absalom's murderous intentions, we can picture David looking back to his days of leading worship in Jerusalem. In the same way, it helps us overcome difficulty when we focus on the things God has done for us in the past. For instance, one of the best things you can do when you have a family argument is to get out the photo album. Look at pictures that bring back memories of God's blessing. It's amazing how the simple act of looking back can change the atmosphere, how restoration is allowed to flow as we recall blessed times together.

God reminded His people again and again of His redeeming act of delivering them from slavery. Moses wrote the first recorded worship song, a hymn of victory, after God parted the Red Sea and destroyed the pharaoh and his army. Many of the psalms focus on God as deliverer and recall instances where He saved His people from calamity. In Psalms 105, 106, and 107 we read lengthy recitations celebrating the Israelites' deliverance. Reciting these psalms reminded the people of what God had already done for them—and therefore what He would do for them again.

David looked forward to seeing God do a similar work of deliverance in his own life. As the king of Israel remembers God's goodness, he lets the Holy Spirit challenge his lagging soul. David revisited God's faithfulness to him and used those memories as a bridge to the future. He cheered himself up by looking back, but then he moved forward. Moving forward is the necessary next step.

I can imagine David's thought process: *All of my past experience shows that God has not withdrawn from me nor abandoned me. So what makes me think He would abandon me now? I will put my hope in God, and I will praise Him once again.* The remedy for David's despair was to turn to God, to thirst after God, and to put his hope in God.

If a dark cloud is covering your life, get ready! God is about to part the clouds and shower you with blessings. If you have learned to find your contentment in obedience to God, and if you trust that God will shine His light into the midst of your darkness, then He will bring peace and restoration.

———◆———

Dear God, in times when I feel alone or abandoned, I will remember Your faithfulness to me. "For you, O LORD, have delivered my soul from death, my eyes from tears, my feet from stumbling." Psalm 116:8

THE JOURNEY OF OBEDIENCE

Just as David was driven from Jerusalem by the murderous plotting of his son, another hero of the Old Testament became an exile not by volunteering for the job, but because it was part of God's plan. Joseph's wandering was forced upon him when his brothers sold him into slavery. But unlike his great-grandfather Abraham, Joseph left his home without the benefit of God's promise that his sojourning was part of a bigger divine scheme.

It's difficult for us to accept that obedience to God would lead to slavery, false accusations, and imprisonment. But all of those happened to Joseph, who remained uncomplaining in his obedience to God. When we read his story, we learn that Joseph was yanked from his home, becoming an exile in Egypt, because God needed him there.

Just as sin and rebellion can create restlessness in our hearts, the opposite can also be true. Obedience to God can result in wandering far from home. Sometimes God wants to see if we will follow Him in obedience, even when we're not aware of the purpose behind it. God calls us out of our comfort zones and into unfamiliar realms.

When Joseph was a teenager, he had dreams of playing a prominent role both in his family and among his people. These dreams stirred a growing awareness that someday he would be used by God. Because Joseph was never secretive about his dreams, his brothers conspired to kill him. Instead of killing him, however, they sold him into slavery (see Genesis 37:12-36).

If we were formulating the path to greatness, most of us would never include these steps: become a slave, get thrown into prison on false charges, and hope that somehow you'll be released. But Joseph endured these injustices year after year. And when the time was right, God elevated Joseph to a position of astounding prominence. Joseph became prime minister of Egypt—second in power only to the pharaoh (see Genesis 43:1-34; 46:1-5).

In retrospect Joseph could see that it was God who had sent him to Egypt. When his family came to Egypt to buy food, Joseph told them, "Do not be distressed and do not be angry with yourselves for selling me here, because it was to save lives that God sent me ahead of you.... You intended to harm me, but God intended it for good" (Genesis 45:5; 50:20).

Thus, Joseph's obedience in following God into slavery, false imprisonment, and eventual greatness preserved his family, the family that eventually grew to become the nation of Israel.

———◆———

Lord, it is my desire to be obedient to You, for I know that You have a unique plan for my life. Show me the path You have set for me. I will seek You with all my heart; do not let me stray from Your commands. See Psalm 119:10

THE PATH OF REDEMPTION

It is important to realize that the restlessness that God stirred in many of the biblical heroes' lives led not only to the redemption of the individual involved but extended to bless untold future generations. In obedience to God, Abraham left his livelihood and his home to become a homeless wanderer. It was through the obedient wandering of Abraham that God set into motion His plan of redemption for humankind.

When he left Mesopotamia, Abram had no destination. God simply told him, "Leave your country, your people and your father's household and go to the land I will show you" (Genesis 12:1). The Lord also promised that He would make a great nation out of Abram's descendants, and changed his name from Abram, meaning "exalted father," to Abraham, "father of a multitude" (see Genesis 17:5). Can you imagine encountering a God who is foreign to your own culture, hearing Him tell you to leave for an undisclosed location, and then doing it? And once you obey that initial command, God changes your name and tells you He will make a mighty nation out of you. You want to believe this part, but you're an old man, and your elderly wife has always been infertile.

Most of us would start questioning our sanity at that point, but Abraham continued to follow God. His sojourn eventually brought him to a city that was destined to be dedicated to the worship of God, a city where people of all nationalities and backgrounds would come in the distant future to learn about the true God.

Abraham first encountered this city when he paid tribute to Melchizedek, the priest-king of Salem, which means "peace." Both the Psalms and the New Testament tell us that Melchizedek, whose name means "king of righteousness," was a type of Christ, our Prince of Peace and King of Righteousness (see Psalm 110:4; Hebrews 5:6-10; 7:1-10). It would be almost a thousand years after Abraham first entered Salem that King David would conquer the city from the Jebusites, and Jerusalem would finally become the center for worship of almighty God.

God had in mind a city where He would be honored and worshiped, a place where people could congregate to learn about Him. With Abraham, and later with David, God made provision for that city. Jerusalem would become known as the City of God. But as glorious as this city was, it was only God's temporary provision, a mere foreshadowing of the Eternal City of God that is still to come.

———◆———

Heavenly Father, give me the faith of Your servant Abraham, who answered Your call without hesitation. Guide me today by Your loving voice and reveal Your will to me. Whether I turn to the right or to the left, let my ears hear Your voice behind me, saying, "This is the way; walk in it." Isaiah 30:21

HONORING GOD

God looked beyond mankind's rebellion and permitted David to set aside a city that would bring glory to God. In spite of—or perhaps because of—his sin, David had a deep desire to revere God. When he repented, David expressed a longing to be in God's presence. "Create in me a pure heart," David implored the Lord, "and renew a steadfast spirit within me. Do not cast me from your presence or take your Holy Spirit from me" (Psalm 51:10-11).

In a sovereign act of grace and election, the Lord honored David's desire to build Jerusalem into a center of worship. God's gracious dealings with David should inspire us all. If your deepest desire is to bring glory to God, then He will overrule the fumbling and stumbling in your life just as He did with David. When you desire to honor the Lord Jesus Christ, God will pour out a blessing on you.

David authored many of the psalms, and when you read his writings, it's obvious just how deeply he delighted in God's presence. The temple musicians used many of David's psalms for public worship—and today the church still sings these psalms. When Solomon dedicated the temple in Jerusalem, the temple his father had dreamed of building, God's glory fell upon the worshipers (see 2 Chronicles 7:1-3). Our inner discontent is often a deep desire to glorify God and to experience His glory in our lives. Wherever God is sought, He will show up in all His glory.

But as much as God manifested His presence in Jerusalem, this city was only God's temporary provision. It was an earthly city, inhabited by people who were far from holy. Years later, when the people of Jerusalem quit seeking God, He departed from His holy temple. In the same way, God will depart from any church where His glory is not sought first and foremost.

Lord, I want to live a life that is honoring to You so that I may enjoy the blessing of uninterrupted fellowship with You. As I seek to honor You, I trust in Your promise: "Those who honor me I will honor, but those who despise me will be disdained." 1 Samuel 2:30

A BLESSING
AND A CONDITION

David and Solomon offered Jerusalem to God as a sacrifice—the sacrifice Cain refused to make—and God accepted it. As long as Israel continued to seek and to worship the true God, the city would enjoy His protection and prosperity.

But after Solomon died, the kingdom split, and gradually the people turned away from God. When the inhabitants of Jerusalem began to worship other gods, the Babylonians were allowed to ransack Jerusalem. They looted and burned the temple and took captive many thousands of the Jewish people.

After more than seventy years of captivity, a remnant of the Jewish people returned. Under the leadership of Zerubbabel, these Jews rebuilt the temple and rededicated their lives to God.

Over time, however, their zeal for the Lord again diminished, and the spiritual vitality of the people of Jerusalem waned.

Finally, at the point when the city rejected its Messiah and became the place of His crucifixion, God rejected earthly Jerusalem as His dwelling place. When the city of God rejected God in human flesh, the city became a corrupted city of man.

Jesus lamented the city's rejection of Him. Yet He did not speak angrily to the citizens of Jerusalem. Instead, He wept hot tears because they had not recognized the day of God's visitation.

Earthly Jerusalem and its temple were only a dim representation of what it means for God to indwell the praises of His people. They were a rough sketch of what can happen when the glory of God is fully revealed. In this life we can't fully comprehend what it means for God to be with us all the time. Why? Because on earth, our discontent often leads us to run away from Him. We tend to forget His commandments and close our ears to His voice. Instead, we are seduced by the voices and the standards of the world system. In the heavenly Jerusalem, however, we will have unending communion with God. There will be no one to whisper doubts and fear and anxiety in our ears, for God's righteousness will have fully restored us.

In the meantime, as we look ahead to the New Jerusalem, we can have intimacy with the God who longs to fellowship with us. When our discontent springs from a burning hunger for God, we will seek Him with our whole hearts, and He will allow us to find Him.

———◆———

"I love those who love me, and those who seek me find me."
Proverbs 8:17

Lord, I love You and I long for the day when I will expe-
rience perfect contentment in Your presence. Show me today
how I can draw closer to You.

PART III

EXPERIENCING GRACE

*But he said to me, "My grace is
sufficient for you, for my power is
made perfect in weakness."*

2 CORINTHIANS 12:9

Coming Home to God

The word *grace,* more than any other word, should constantly amaze us. There is perhaps no more powerful depiction of God's amazing grace than the story of the prodigal son. In this story we witness the repentant return of a wayward son into the arms of a grace-filled father. God's welcoming grace is the place where discontent begins to fade.

Unlike Joseph and Abraham, whose sojourns began in obedience to either God's call or His intervention, the prodigal son left home out of willfulness. He insisted on getting what was his, turning his back on his father. The loving father could only watch his son's figure grow smaller and smaller and then disappear in the distance.

But the son eventually reached a turning point, and the story has a joyous ending. Unlike Cain and Nimrod, who refused to repent and turn back to God, the prodigal son ended his sinful wandering when he reached the end of himself. It was then that he recalled his father's love and care, and he returned home as a broken, repentant son.

If you have trouble relating to the accomplishments of biblical heroes and heroines, then think of your life in light of the prodigal son. He was an ordinary person who showed no great courage and was never a great leader. But he did remember his father when his wandering fed him the bitter fruit that comes from disobedience. Most of us can identify with the prodigal son who brought despair and humiliation on himself.

Like this young man, we may find ourselves wandering far from the Father who loves us. Often we recognize that we're putting distance between ourselves and God, but still we continue on our way. The glorious news in Scripture is that while we experiment with life apart from God, He patiently waits for us to return. And He welcomes us home with the joy and warm embrace that we see in this grace-filled story.

Father, "I have strayed like a lost sheep. Seek your servant, for I have not forgotten your commands." Psalm 119:176

Dear Lord, I place my trust in You because You have made me alive in Christ even when I was dead in my transgressions. By Your grace You have promised to save me. See Ephesians 2:5

THE GIFT OF GRACE

The free gift of God's grace goes against every human instinct and every other religious system. The Buddhist eightfold path, the Hindu doctrine of karma, the Jewish ceremonial law, and the Islamic shari'ah law all require followers to earn divine approval. Only Jesus Christ, through whom the world was created, offers unconditional love. Only God in human flesh could be so extravagant in His generosity.

But why would God continue to offer us His free gift of grace, especially after we rebel and wander far from Him? God's nature won't allow Him to do anything other than to pursue those who are lost. Most in our society are more interested in exercising their rights than they are in God's grace. In a world with civil rights, gay rights, and even animal rights, grace hardly seems necessary. Most people believe they can be good on their own, without relying on God.

We are aware of the continuing search for a better life, for peace and fulfillment. But we fail to see that the only hope for our restoration is God and His grace.

Scripture describes two types of grace. The first is what theologians refer to as "common grace," but more accurately it should be called "mercy," which is freely given to everyone. God "causes his sun to rise on the evil and the good, and sends rain on the righteous and the unrighteous" (Matthew 5:45). The beauty of God's creation is free for everyone to enjoy, whether they follow God or not.

In contrast to God's mercy, however, His grace is given exclusively to those who belong to Christ. This grace is lavished only upon those who have accepted the sacrifice of God's Son and received Him as their Savior and Lord. This grace is the unmerited, inexhaustible, and irresistible favor of God. This is the grace that restores us—satisfying our longing for contentment. To constantly revel in the God of grace and the grace of God is the most exhilarating aspect of the Christian life.

"And God is able to make all grace abound to you, so that in all things at all times, having all that you need, you will abound in every good work." 2 Corinthians 9:8

Lord, I praise You for Your unending goodness to me. When I begin to feel restless, I will stop and consider the undeserved favor You have bestowed upon me.

PART IV

Steps Toward Contentment

*I have told you these things, so that
in me you may have peace. In this world
you will have trouble. But take heart!
I have overcome the world.*

John 16:33

CONFRONTING
OUR WEAKNESSES

As we fall gladly into God's welcoming arms and set our feet on a new path, we need to be aware of attitudes, habits, and circumstances that can send us off-course. If we're not aware of these detours, we'll lose the peace and contentment of God. The first detour we need to recognize is that of personal weaknesses.

In 2 Corinthians, God makes the promise to the apostle Paul, "My grace is sufficient for you, for My strength is made perfect in weakness" (12:9, NKJV). We all go through times when we're trying to move ahead in life, but just as we pull into the passing lane to get around an eighteen-wheeler, another truck comes roaring down the highway from the opposite direction. We're just trying to make progress, but we're staring imminent danger right in the eyes—or right in the headlights, as the case may be.

At some point, life beats us down. It might be the loss of a loved one, a doctor's terrifying diagnosis, or the betrayal of a friend. Whenever these threats bear down on us, we can either rely on our own resources or we can admit our helplessness and draw on the outpouring of God's grace.

We most readily recognize our need for God when we are the weakest. The weaker we become, the more we pray. And the more we pray, the more God's strength is made perfect in our weakness.

The apostle Paul faced the threatening rush of human weakness and begged God to remove the weakness. Paul had been given a "thorn in the flesh," a constant reminder of his human frailty. Whatever Paul's thorn was, we know it was no minor irritation.

It is no accident that God the Holy Spirit, who authored the Scriptures, did not specify what Paul's problem was. By not knowing the exact nature of his suffering, we can all imagine Paul hurting with whatever hurts us. And as we limp along in our human frailty, we can identify with Paul's initial longing for God to remove the thorn.

———◆———

Father, it's difficult for me to confront my weaknesses. Human pride tempts me to deny my frailty and my flaws. But in light of Your promise to be my strength, I confess my shortcomings. Help me to place my confidence only in You so that I may say with Paul, "If I must boast, I will boast of the things that show my weakness." 2 Corinthians 11:30

THE TRUTH ABOUT THORNS

As you confront the thorns in your life, keep in mind their potential to detour you from the path of contentment. Even those who pursue the peace that comes from God's grace can get tripped up when they encounter painful circumstances.

To avoid the detours, keep in mind three biblical truths.

Satan is the manufacturer of thorns. Paul described his thorn as "a messenger of Satan" that had been sent to torment him (2 Corinthians 12:7). Satan never sends you love messages. His messages, and the vehicle he uses as his messenger, will always put dread in your heart. Identifying Satan as the source helps us put our thorns in perspective.

God's grace takes away the sting. Don't allow Satan's torments to make you doubt that God will bring good out of bad. Don't permit Satan to convince you that God doesn't love you enough to give you grace for every moment. Whatever thorns are causing you to suffer, God is using them for your own protection. You may be weary of the thorns, but be assured that God can take away the sting.

God's grace brings roses out of thorns. Paul did not ask for grace, but God gave him grace anyway. Grace is the spiritual power to live triumphantly no matter what our circumstances. It is the spiritual ability to see the rose that is about to blossom in the midst of the briar patch.

Grace always shines the brightest against the darkness of our circumstances. If God's grace is not sufficient for you, then it may be that you are focusing so much on the thorn that you can't see the rose of God's grace developing in you. Once our concerns are left at the feet of our Lord, we must then trust that His grace is entirely sufficient. Apart from trusting in God's grace, there is no peace, no rest, and no contentment.

———◆———

Father God, I know that You are not the author of the pain and trials that torment me. Instead, these things are fiery darts from the Enemy. When I become discouraged, help me remember that Your grace is completely sufficient for all of my needs. See 2 Corinthians 12:9

THE LIE OF LEGALISM

If we are on a journey to God's heart, finding contentment in His love and acceptance, legalism can detour us onto paths that lead far from the Lord. Legalism propagates the error that salvation comes through God's grace *plus* our effort.

Paul wrote his letter to the Christians in Galatia to combat the false doctrine of legalism—the faulty notion that God's grace is merely a beginning and that continuing the journey of the Christian life requires the force of our own effort.

It's the fallacy that salvation becomes effective through grace *plus* something else: believing a certain religious dogma, practicing a ritual or sacrament, performing certain good deeds, the avoidance of certain behaviors, or peculiarities of outward appearance, such as requiring that women wear a head covering. In simple terms, legalism is the elevation of man-made rules to the level of God's commands.

I grew up in legalism and have experienced firsthand its power to steal our joy in living and walking daily in the presence of Christ. When you begin to bask in the sunshine of God's grace, you will never go back to legalism. And I guarantee that you will not miss that joyless way of living.

The Word of God points out the lie of legalism. We are saved by God's grace alone, through faith alone, and even that faith is not our own; it is God's gift to us. We were dead in our sins, incapable of belief, until God breathed His faith into our lives.

Lord, thank You that Your grace alone is sufficient to save me. The man-made requirements of legalism are of no benefit. When Jesus came, redundant rituals were nullified: "The law was given through Moses; grace and truth came through Jesus Christ." John 1:17

BLESSED ASSURANCE

Legalists often tell their followers that if they fail to adhere to certain man-made requirements and prohibitions, they are in danger of losing their salvation. This is often referred to as falling from grace. But such use of this phrase creates confusion.

Believing that a Christian can forfeit his or her salvation runs contrary to the words of Jesus: "All that the Father gives me will come to me, and whoever comes to me I will never drive away.... And this is the will of him who sent me, that I shall lose none of all that he has given me, but raise them up at the last day" (John 6:37,39).

It's tragic that many Christians lack joy, peace, and hope simply because they don't know if they will go to heaven. But God tells us that we *can* be sure of our salvation. God finishes what He starts, and His grace is "able to keep you from falling and to present you before his glorious presence without fault and with great joy" (Jude 24).

If Paul did not use the expression "fallen from grace" to mean that a Christian could lose his or her salvation, what did he mean? It's clear from the context that he was talking about legalism. Notice what he wrote: "You who are trying to be justified by law have been alienated from Christ; you have fallen away from grace" (Galatians 5:4).

To sin and then to repent and ask for God's grace in forgiveness is not falling from grace. But relying on your own ability to adhere to certain rules and rituals as the basis of your righteousness is a clear step away from God's grace. Choosing legalism is abandoning grace as the basis of our relationship with God, or falling from grace. Don't trust your own efforts. Place your trust only in the all-sufficient work of Christ in salvation.

———◆———

Lord, I realize that I can have assurance of my salvation. In spite of my inherited sin nature, my eternal future is secure because of the sacrifice made on the Cross by Jesus Christ. "In him we have redemption through his blood, the forgiveness of sins, in accordance with the riches of God's grace." Ephesians 1:7

GRACE MISUNDERSTOOD

Scripture reminds us that because we all are sinners, there is nothing we can do to earn God's grace. However, many people have gone to the other extreme of legalism by interpreting God's grace as a license to sin. There are those who ask, Can't we freely break every commandment without suffering any consequences? If we've received salvation, we'll still go to heaven, won't we?

Asking this question demonstrates that a person has not had a direct encounter with God's grace. If you believe you have the right to ignore God's commandments, you are not saved. Paul warned the Christians of Galatia not to use the liberty of God's grace as a license to sin. He wrote, "Do not use your freedom to indulge the sinful nature; rather, serve one another in love" (Galatians 5:13).

Although we are not saved by keeping the law, the Bible tells us that those who have been saved by grace *do* keep God's commandments. A person who has experienced God's grace does not just obey the commandment not to covet his neighbor's possessions, he follows Christ in loving his neighbor sacrificially. But Christians are not left to do this alone. The Holy Spirit empowers us to do what is not humanly possible, to live in obedience to God.

God's grace provides the desire and gives us the power to obey Him. Relying on our own ability to fulfill rules and regulations creates anxiety that steals our peace. The path to God is the path of grace, which leads to peace and contentment. Legalism will set us on a path of wandering away from God rather than the path of trust in His grace. Don't take the detour. Don't trade the peace of returning to God for the bondage of legalism.

———◆———

I never want to take Your precious gift of grace for granted, Lord. I do not want to be like the wicked who "do not learn righteousness; even in a land of uprightness they go on doing evil and regard not the majesty of the LORD." Isaiah 26:10

Father, help me walk in the freedom and obedience of a growing relationship with You.

THE ENEMY OF PRAYER

Restlessness is not always a consequence of disobedience. Our discontent can come from God, as a prompting that He wants us to make a change, to shift direction, or to take a stand. But if we start feeling that we deserve better, or that God is somehow short-changing us, and decide to shift directions in an effort to find contentment on our own, we are probably following our sinful nature.

Human pride resides within all of us, since we all have inherited a sin nature. Not only is pride a powerful force, it is also deceptive. We can talk ourselves into believing that our choices are motivated by a desire to do good when, in fact, we are motivated by a desire to do what's best for ourselves. Setting aside our own agenda starts with accepting God's invitation to come boldly before His throne of grace. With such an invitation extended to us, how can we possibly neglect the pursuit of prayer? Part of the problem is that life can become too comfortable.

Ask the average Christian how long he or she spends in personal prayer time when everything is going well. You'll probably be met with a sheepish look and a good deal of hemming and hawing. Some Christians are consistent in prayer, but most are crisis prayer warriors. The Enemy of our souls knows that prayer is the source of our strength. Therefore, Satan does all that is within his power to cut our supply lines. If the Enemy can keep us from praying, he can block God's outpouring of blessing on our lives.

And aside from the Enemy's distraction tactics, perhaps the biggest enemy of prayer is pride. Pride tells us that we can solve any problem, accomplish anything we set our mind to. We let ourselves believe that everything we need can be achieved through human effort, if we just invest enough time and enough energy. That sounds logical, but it's a lie. It's no wonder we get into such desperate spiritual trouble when we neglect prayer.

Lord, at times I have fallen for the Enemy's distractions and not called out to You in prayer. I confess that as sin. But other times I have not prayed because I didn't know how to express my feelings to You. Today I claim Your promise that Your Holy Spirit "helps us in our weakness. We do not know what we ought to pray for, but the Spirit himself intercedes for us with groans that words cannot express." Romans 8:26

THE PRIVILEGE OF PRAYER

Many of us neglect our prayer lives because we don't comprehend the awesome privilege of praying. We simply do not understand God's eagerness to answer our prayers. And we fail to appreciate the power of connectedness with the Almighty that comes through prayer.

In a time of grave crisis, Queen Esther approached the king's throne in fear. It was against the law to come before the king without his invitation. Had the king not extended the royal scepter, signifying his willingness to grant her an audience, Esther could have been put to death. But the king was pleased to see her, even though she appeared unannounced and uninvited.

If a human king could extend grace to an uninvited visitor, how much more is God willing to extend grace to us when we approach Him in prayer? After all, we have an explicit invitation to come before God's throne and to beseech Him for whatever we need.

Here is the amazing invitation God has extended to us:

> Therefore, since we have a great high priest who has gone through the heavens, Jesus the Son of God, let us hold firmly to the faith we profess. For we do not have a high priest who is unable to sympathize with our weaknesses, but we have one who has been tempted in every way, just as we are—yet was without sin. Let us then approach the throne of grace with confidence, so that we may receive mercy and find grace to help us in our time of need. (Hebrews 4:14-16)

We need not approach God in fear, worrying whether He will receive us. When we have accepted Christ as our Savior, we are invited to enter the royal throne room. We have a right to be there, and it is our privilege to pour our hearts out to God. All who are followers of the Lord Jesus Christ are invited to experience the awesomeness of the power of the grace of God in prayer.

———◆———

What an amazing privilege it is to come to You in prayer, Father. Your Word tells me that I can approach You with confidence. I know that if I ask anything according to Your will, You will hear me. "And if we know that he hears us— whatever we ask—we know that we have what we asked of him." 1 John 5:15

APPROACHING GOD
IN PRAYER

Esther approached a human king, hoping for grace but knowing that the judgment of death could await her instead. In contrast, when we approach the throne of the King of the Universe, He *always* gives us grace.

The writer of Hebrews invites all who have put their trust in Jesus Christ to draw near to God's throne with confidence. If you try to come on your own merits, you won't have confidence that your prayers will be heard. But if you come trusting in nothing but what Jesus has done for you, if you come with confidence only because of the shedding of Christ's blood for you, then you will find grace in times of need.

The throne of grace represents the seat of God's unmerited favor and kindness toward us. The throne signifies His unlimited forgiveness and the blessings, power, and strength He extends to us. If you are distraught and fearful, or confused and anxious, there is comfort, wisdom, and discernment for you at God's throne. If you are discouraged and about to give up, there is encouragement for you at the throne. If you are weak and defeated, there is victory for you at the throne of grace.

When we pray, we often feel our prayers are falling on deaf ears. We must approach God's throne on the basis of Christ's shed blood, and we must ask the King for help. "You do not have, because you do not ask God," James wrote. "When you ask, you do not receive, because you ask with wrong motives, that you may spend what you get on your pleasures" (James 4:2-3).

When we begin to understand God's awesome grace and mercy, running to the throne of grace will become a regular habit. God has promised that we will find help. And when we make prayer the pattern of our lives, we will learn to extend the comfort and strength we find to others who are struggling (see Hebrews 10:19-24).

———◆———

"And God is able to make all grace abound to you, so that in all things at all times, having all that you need, you will abound in every good work." 2 Corinthians 9:8

Lord, I know that whatever my needs may be, I can confidently bring them to You in prayer. Your loving eyes are on me, Your ears are open to my cry. You will always deliver me from my troubles. See Psalm 34:15,17

DON'T MISS THE BLESSING

When Jesus told the story of the widow's mite, He commended the woman's generosity because He could see her heart. She gave out of her poverty, and she gave sacrificially. Her meager gift meant more to her, and to the Lord, because it was given out of scarcity.

But most Americans don't have to choose between buying food or giving a gift to God. We can donate a portion of our income and still have plenty to live on. But even though we enjoy material comfort, most people fail to give generously. The level of comfort we experience can work against a healthy restlessness that drives us to give back to God a portion of what He has given to us.

The widow whose story is told in the gospel of Luke experienced some of that internal restlessness as she waited to give her gift at the temple. For one, she regretted that she was not able to give more. But she barely had enough money to cover basic, survival-level needs. And to avoid having more shame heaped upon her, she waited until others dispersed before she gave her small offering. But Jesus was still there, and He knew the woman's generosity. The unease she felt internally was born of her desire to give even more.

To those who struggle for survival like the widow, even a little seems like a lot. In contrast, having more than we need often brings with it a false sense that we can take credit for our material well-being. We forget to give thanks because we're too comfortable. Affluence can quiet the healthy restlessness that draws us to rely on God's provision. If we keep accepting the gracious gifts of our heavenly Father—taking and taking without giving back and expressing heartfelt gratitude—before long we'll become spoiled brats, spiritually speaking.

In addition to verbally expressing our thanks to God, one of the best ways we can demonstrate our gratitude is through our giving. Jesus said, "Where your money is, there you will find your heart" (Matthew 6:21, author's paraphrase). Note that He did not single out preaching or teaching or any other highly visible ministry involvement. Instead, He made it clear that how you spend your money demonstrates where your heart is. Many Christians need a spiritual heart transplant because their giving records show that their heart is in the wrong place.

———◆———

Lord God, "From the fullness of [Your] grace we have all received one blessing after another." John 1:16

I am so thankful for the gifts You have given me. Help me show my gratitude to You by giving back to You and to others.

EXEMPLARY GIVING

The Corinthians were prosperous people. They were also proud of their biblical sophistication and boasted of their spirituality. So when Paul told them about an urgent need facing the church in Jerusalem, where the followers of Christ were being persecuted, the Corinthians made the largest financial pledge of all the churches. But when the time came to collect the offering, it was a different story.

Evidently the Corinthians were slow to complete their pledge, so in 2 Corinthians 8–9, Paul gently taught this prosperous church about the grace of giving. In two chapters, he mentioned grace six times. He taught the Corinthians that those who have received much must give much—not as payment for their salvation but as an expression of thankfulness to God. He delights in receiving our thanks and is pleased when we express our appreciation through the grace of giving.

When you experience a time of feasting in your life and you give God the crumbs off your plate, that doesn't honor Him. But when you're facing the possibility of famine and you make a sacrificial gift, you are honoring God. When everything is falling apart and you give sacrificially, you are learning the grace of giving.

The normal human reaction when we're going through trials is to ignore the suffering of others. We're tempted to think, *I can barely pay my own bills. I just can't help anybody else.* Recalling the widow at the temple, however, we realize this is not the attitude of those who have freely received the grace of God. Grace givers understand that problems are simply a part of life. They should have no bearing on our giving.

In times of difficulty, grace givers actually become more sensitive to the pain of others, more patient with those who are struggling, more willing to help financially. Grace givers allow their trials to move them to minister to others with compassion.

———

Heavenly Father, at times it is difficult for me to give, so I pray that You would change my heart. Help me fathom Your incredible promise: " 'Bring the whole tithe into the storehouse, that there may be food in my house. Test me in this,' says the LORD Almighty, 'and see if I will not throw open the floodgates of heaven and pour out so much blessing that you will not have room enough for it.' " Malachi 3:10

BECOMING A GRACE GIVER

In 2 Corinthians we read that out of their most severe trial, the Macedonian Christians overflowed with joy, and they expressed that joy by giving. What could have made them joyful when they were facing such severe trials? They took joy in the fact that God's grace had found them, that they had been brought out of the darkness of paganism into the light of Christ. The joy of their salvation overflowed into the joy of giving.

The grace of giving is never an obligation, like paying income taxes. If you view giving to God as a burden or an obligation, then you are missing out on the overflowing joy that comes from being a "hilarious" giver (see 2 Corinthians 9:7). The word translated *cheerful* in this verse is the Greek word *hilaros,* which has the connotation of exuberance and merriment. Grace giving is *hilarious* giving, and it is those who give with hilarity whom God loves.

The amount of our gifts may be quite small, but our gifts can appear large in the eyes of God. As God measures our giving, a large gift is a gift of any amount that is given sacrificially. In addition, the sacrifice has to be made freely. Grace givers learn to be hilarious givers, and in return they receive an outpouring of God's blessings.

When you follow the example of hilarious giving, all your needs will be met and you will have adequate resources to continue investing in God's work (see 2 Corinthians 9:8,11). Living in grace and giving in grace go hand in hand. Those who have received much must give much as an expression of gratitude to God. Indeed, generous giving is an unseen source of contentment even in the midst of trials.

———◆———

Dear Lord, help me become a grace giver. I want to heed the advice of the apostle Paul who encourages us, "But just as you excel in everything—in faith, in speech, in knowledge, in complete earnestness and in your love for us—see that you also excel in this grace of giving." 2 Corinthians 8:7

PART V

THE END
OF OUR DISCONTENT

*In my Father's house are many rooms; if it
were not so, I would have told you. I am
going there to prepare a place for you.
And if I go and prepare a place for you,
I will come back and take you to be with
me that you also may be where I am.*

JOHN 14:2-3

THE ULTIMATE PLACE OF REST

In the first few devotions of this book, we looked at the loss of contentment that steals peace from our hearts and leads to destructive attempts to quiet our restlessness. We have also seen that true peace comes only through God's grace. The highest experience of peace and contentment is found in the life of obedience to God.

Still, earthly peace and contentment are but dim shadows of what is to come. A day looms in the future when God will judge the world so He can establish the heavenly Jerusalem, where His children will enjoy the Lord's presence forever.

God began human history in a paradise known as the Garden of Eden, where the first humans enjoyed unhindered fellowship with God. Likewise, God will close earthly history with a garden city, a heavenly city known as the New Jerusalem. In that city, we will dwell with Him for eternity. And that, at long last, will put an end to our longing for more.

In the book of Revelation, we read about the permanent dwelling place for everyone who has placed their faith in Christ. In this promised garden city, we will be fully restored to the intimate communion with God for which we were created. At long last, our wandering will end.

When Adam and Eve were evicted from the Garden of Eden, humanity began looking for a city. Cain and his descendants foolishly sought a home in the rebellious city of man. But God promises a heavenly city, the place that Abraham looked forward to, "the city with foundations, whose architect and builder is God" (Hebrews 11:10). This city of God has foundations, which implies permanence, and for that reason we often refer to it as the eternal city.

The ancient city of Jerusalem foreshadowed "the city that is to come" (Hebrews 13:14). The Bible also refers to this future city as "the heavenly Jerusalem" (Hebrews 12:22) and "the Holy City, the new Jerusalem" (Revelation 21:2; 3:12). Earthly Jerusalem was considered a holy city because God allowed Solomon to build a "home" for Him there. From that time forward, the temple became the focal point for worshiping God in the Hebrew faith. But as Christians, *we* have now become the temples of the Holy Spirit (see 1 Corinthians 6:19). There is no longer a need for an earthly temple because the ultimate sacrifice for sin has been offered once and for all in Jesus.

Sometimes we struggle so hard to keep the proper perspective between the earthly realm and the eternal that we lose an awareness of our heavenly future. Heaven is not just a far-off vacation spot we will visit some day. As believers in Christ, we are *already* citizens of heaven—and when you look at it that way, life on planet Earth is nothing more than a short layover before we enter our heavenly home.

———◆———

What a blessing it is, Lord, to rest assured in the knowledge that You give eternal life; no one can snatch me from Your hand. See John 10:28

Help me see my life on earth in the proper perspective as I look forward to the ultimate place of peace—my heavenly home.

OUR HEAVENLY HOME

The Bible tells us that our heavenly home offers beauty beyond comprehension along with a permanent end to our restlessness. Why, then, are Christians apt to forget that ultimate contentment comes from God and that we will never fully experience rest and peace until we enter heaven? I believe there are five reasons people seek contentment in the things of earth rather than the things of God.

False perceptions. Most of us fail to dwell on the magnificent glory of heaven. Many think heaven is populated by blond-haired, chubby-cheeked, greeting-card cherubs. As we have seen, that image bears no resemblance to the majesty and glory of the city that needs neither sun nor moon because God Himself is its light (see Revelation 21:23).

Life's pressures. The emotional wear and tear of life can steal our attention away from eternal matters. But the Lord wants us to be faithful even while we face demanding responsibilities. He wants us to serve Him in all we do so that we can draw the attention of the world to the Savior. We must let people know that we live the way we do because we have a home in heaven and that they, too, may be forgiven and enjoy eternity in the New Jerusalem.

The allure of what is seen. Whatever we see gets our immediate attention. Heaven is "out of sight," therefore it remains "out of mind." We tend to believe what is verifiable, and we prefer to verify things visually. Then we fall into the trap of believing that the life we can see will go on forever, so we invest everything we have in this life.

The church's worldliness. The early church measured success in terms of eternal gain, not membership growth or financial prosperity. But today many people preach health and wealth here on earth. Why would anyone spend time thinking about heaven if they believe they can get everything they want right here?

False doctrine. The majority of Americans think they will automatically go to heaven when they die. And amazingly, many churches are teaching that God saves everyone. The truth is that there *is* a literal hell, but those who end up there are not sent there by God. Those who enter hell send themselves there by refusing God's provision for their salvation.

God woos us, longing to hold us in His embrace. Our lack of satisfaction in life, our restlessness, our loss of peace—all of these should bring us to the end of ourselves where we will finally turn and seek God's grace.

Our home, our place of rest and contentment, is with God.

Lord, there are so many distractions in the world. Please help me focus less on that which is temporal and more on what is everlasting. For You have instructed Your children saying, "Do not work for food that spoils, but for food that endures to eternal life, which the Son of Man will give you." John 6:27

A Special Invitation

God has "set eternity in the hearts of men," Solomon tells us in Ecclesiastes 3:11. Our nagging sense that things just aren't right can become the driving force to bring us into a personal relationship with God or bring us back to God if we have known Him but have wandered away. Because we are made in God's image, something inside tells us there is more than what we see in the physical world, more than what we can comprehend through our rational minds.

We are pushed to the limit by the demands of modern life, leaving us weary and distraught. We are hounded by regret, we are worried, and often we are filled with anxiety. Even those who don't recognize this dis-ease as a spiritual issue are familiar with the crying need for rest, peace, and security. Discontent is a spiritual issue that requires a spiritual solution, and God alone can restore us, providing what we hunger for.

God's deliverance and care bring rest to the soul:

The LORD is gracious and righteous;
    our God is full of compassion.
The LORD protects the simplehearted;
    when I was in great need, he saved me.
Be at rest once more, O my soul,
    for the LORD has been good to you. (Psalm 116:5-7)

God intended rest to be a part of the natural rhythm of life. On the seventh day of Creation, the Sabbath day, our Creator rested from all His labor. He designed rest into the spiritual realm as well, holding out rest as the destination and satisfaction of our spiritual longing. Humankind's restless discontent is a search for the rest promised by the Lord, the rest that brings peace and repose to our troubled hearts. Only when our wandering leads us home to the Father will we find the peace and contentment that we seek.

God continues to extend the invitation: "The promise of entering his rest still stands.... There remains, then, a Sabbath-rest for the people of God" (Hebrews 4:1,9). My prayer is that you will accept God's invitation and enter into the rest that only He offers—starting in this life and continuing for eternity in the life to come.

To learn more about WaterBrook Press and view
our catalog of products, log on to our Web site:
www.waterbrookpress.com

WATERBROOK
PRESS